The MAILBOX®
The Education Center®

grades
PreK–K

D1474470

Alphabet Puppets
From A to Z

Build a strong foundation for reading success!

- Early Literacy Concepts
- Phonological Awareness
- Letter Recognition
- Letter-Sound Association
- General Alphabet Knowledge

Kiki K. Kite

Written by Ada Goren

Managing Editor: Kimberly Brugger-Murphy

Editorial Team: Becky S. Andrews, Diane Badden, Kimberley Bruck, Karen A. Brudnak, Kitty Campbell, Pam Crane, Lynette Dickerson, Sarah Foreman, Theresa Lewis Goode, Tazmen Hansen, Marsha Heim, Lori Z. Henry, Debra Liverman, Dorothy C. McKinney, Thad H. McLaurin, Brenda Miner, Sharon Murphy, Jennifer Nunn, Mark Rainey, Greg D. Rieves, Hope Rodgers, Eliseo De Jesus Santos II, Donna K. Teal

www.themailbox.com

©2008 The Mailbox® Books
All rights reserved.
ISBN10 #1-56234-799-3 • ISBN13 #978-156234-799-4

Manufactured in the United States
10 9 8 7 6 5 4 3 2 1

Table of Contents

What's Inside

Easy-to-follow instructions

A mini poster for each letter

Two activities per letter

Timesaving patterns

Aggie A. Alligator

Materials for one puppet:

copy of page 7
copy of the name card on page 8
paper lunch bag
crayons
scissors
glue

Aggie A. Alligator

Directions

1. Color the puppet patterns.
2. Cut out the patterns and the name card.
3. Glue the cutouts to the bag, as shown, to make the puppet.

4 *Alphabet Puppets From A to Z* • ©The Mailbox® Books • TEC61113

Aggie A. Alligator

Aggie A. Alligator
Loves apple pie.
She sees one and she says,
"My, oh my!"
She opens her mouth,
And in one big bite,
That sweet apple pie
Is gone from sight!

Aa

Alphabet Puppets From A to Z • ©The Mailbox® Books • TEC61113 **5**

Sweet Apple Pie
Initial sound /ă/

For this group-time activity, mount a copy of each picture card from page 8 on a die-cut apple shape and put the apples in a basket. Obtain a pie tin and cut and decorate a brown construction paper piecrust to fit the top of the tin. Don your Aggie A. Alligator puppet. Then have Aggie ask a volunteer to pick an apple from the basket. Use Aggie to engage little ones in naming the picture and its beginning sound. If the word begins with the /ă/ sound, have the volunteer put the apple in the pie tin while Aggie displays enthusiastic approval! If the apple shows a word that does not begin with the /ă/ sound, have her put it to the side while Aggie gives a disappointed sigh. After all of the apples with the /ă/ sound have been put in the pie tin, cover the tin with the piecrust. Then invite Aggie to gobble up the appetizing pie!

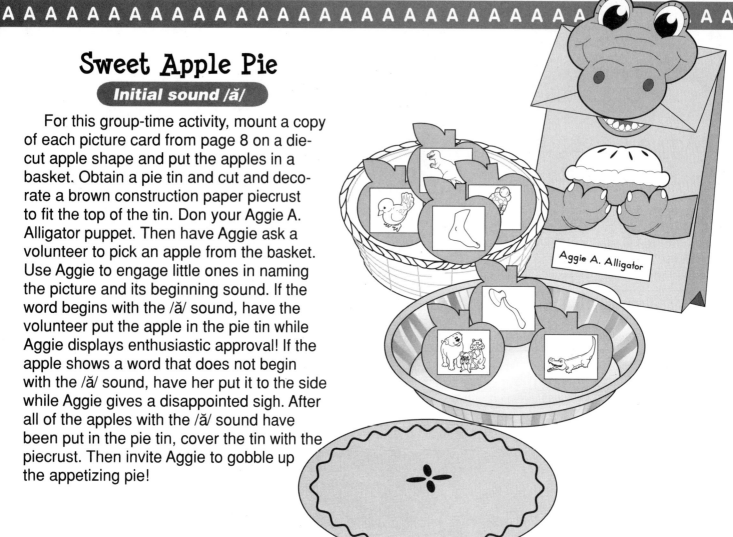

Aggie A. Alligator

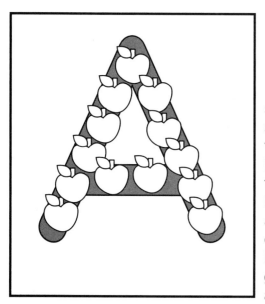

Aggie Loves Apples!
Letter-sound association

In advance, cut two apples in half lengthwise and prepare shallow containers of red, yellow, and green paint. Give each student a sheet of construction paper displaying an outline of the letter *A*. Don your Aggie A. Alligator puppet. Have Aggie instruct each child to dip an apple in a color of his choice and then stamp the apple inside the outline. As youngsters work, have Aggie lead them in chanting, "/ă/, /ă/, /ă/, /ă/, Aggie loves apples!" Use Aggie A. Alligator to encourage little learners to continue until the letter is covered with prints. After the paint has dried, have each child draw stems on her apple prints and glue on construction paper leaves. Post the completed projects along with Aggie A. Alligator for all to see!

Name Card

Use with "Aggie A. Alligator" on page 4.

Aggie A. Alligator

Picture Cards

Use with "Sweet Apple Pie" on page 6.

Alphabet Puppets From A to Z • ©The Mailbox® Books • TEC61113

Bubbles B. Bear

Materials for one puppet:

copy of page 12
lunch bag
crayons
scissors
glue

Bubbles B. Bear

Directions

1. Color the puppet patterns.
2. Cut out the patterns and the name card.
3. Glue the cutouts to the bag to make the puppet shown.

Bubbles B. Bear

Bubbles B. Bear

Is a clean little cub.

Every night Bubbles

Hops in the tub.

He eats up the soap,

He burps bubbles galore,

And then he says, "Thanks!

May I please have some more?"

Bb

Ask Bubbles
Initial sound /b/

Collect an assortment of items that begin with /b/. Put the items in a box along with items that do not begin with /b/. Cut a large bubble shape from cellophane or paper and label the bubble "Bb." Use your Bubbles B. Bear puppet to introduce the box. Lead students in reciting the first two lines of the chant shown. Have your Bubbles puppet respond with the final two lines, inserting a child's name when indicated. Have the child remove one item from the box. Use the puppet to engage students in naming the item and evaluating its beginning sound. If the item begins with /b/, have the child put it inside the bubble cutout. If it does not, have him set the item aside. Continue in this manner until the box is empty.

Students: Bubbles, Bubbles,
What's in the box?
Bubbles: [Child's name, child's name], look and see.
/b/, /b/, /b/! Does it start with *B?*

A Very Big *B*
Letter-sound association

Have Bubbles B. Bear cheer little learners on during this group activity. Prepare a large outline of the letter *B* and provide colorful stamp pads and a supply of rubber or foam *B* stamps. Each youngster, in turn, inks a rubber stamp and stamps the letter *B* inside the outline. During each child's turn, have Bubbles lead the group in chanting, "/b/, /b/, /b/!" Cut out the finished artwork. Then display the letter cutout with a Bubbles B. Bear puppet for an impressive reminder of the letter *B* and the sound it makes.

Puppet Patterns and Name Card
Use with "Bubbles B. Bear" on page 9.

Bubbles B. Bear

 **oco C. Cookie**

CCCCCCCCCCCCCCCCCCCCCCCCCCCCCCCCCCCCCC

Materials for one puppet:

copy of the puppet pattern on page 16
2 paper plates
crayons
scissors
glue
stapler

Coco C. Cookie

Directions

1. Color and cut out the bathing suit pattern; then glue the cutout to the outside of a paper plate.
2. Draw a face on the plate.
3. Draw chocolate chips on both paper plates.
4. Staple the two plates together, leaving at the bottom an opening large enough for your hand to fit through.

CCCCCCCCCCCCCCCCCCCCCCCCCCCCCCCCC

Coco C. Cookie

Coco C. Cookie

Is very cute!

She likes to wear

Her bathing suit.

In a cup of milk,

She'll swim and splash

And then dry on a napkin

In a flash!

CCCCCCCCCCCCCCCCCCCCCCCCCCCCCCCC

Coco's Favorite Chips

Initial hard sound of the letter C

In advance, cut a large cookie shape from poster board. Cut out the chips from a copy of page 17 and place them facedown on a cookie tray. Slide your Coco C. Cookie puppet on your hand. Then have Coco invite little ones to help her decorate this colossal cookie! Prompt a volunteer to choose a chip and name the picture. If its name begins with the /k/ sound of the letter *C,* have the student place the chip on the cookie. If it does not, have him set the chip aside. Continue in this manner until the tray is empty. Once the cookie is complete, have Coco lead youngsters in reviewing the words.

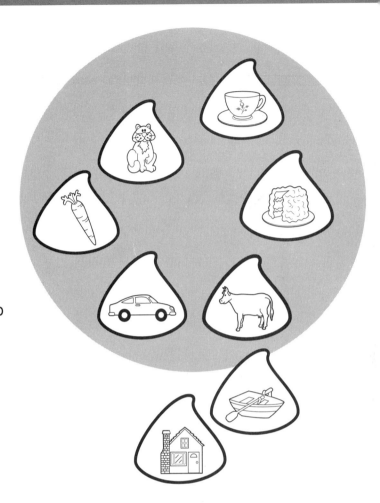

C Is for Cookies

Forming letter C

All of this talk about cookies is bound to make youngsters hungry! Give each child a napkin, a cup of milk, a spoon, and a handful of miniature cookie snacks or cereal. Have your puppet instruct each child to arrange the miniature cookies on her napkin to form the letter *C.* Then have Coco invite each child to put her cookies in her cup of milk and let them go for a swim—just as Coco did! Finally, invite her to use her spoon to eat the tasty cookies!

Puppet Pattern
Use with "Coco C. Cookie" on page 13.

Coco C. Cookie

TEC61113

Alphabet Puppets From A to Z • ©The Mailbox® Books • TEC61113

TEC61113

TEC61113

TEC61113

TEC61113

TEC61113

TEC61113

TEC61113

TEC61113

Doodle D. Dog

D D D D D D D D D D D D D D D D D D D D D D D D D D D D D D

Materials for one puppet:

copies of the puppet pattern and
    name card on page 21 and the
    puppet patterns on page 22
paper lunch bag
crayons
scissors
glue

Doodle D. Dog

Directions

1. Color the puppet patterns.
2. Cut out the patterns and the name card.
3. Cut along the dotted lines.
4. Glue the cutouts to the bag, as shown, to make the puppet.

Doodle D. Dog

Doodle D. Dog just loves to draw.

There's always a crayon in his paw.

He draws daisies and ducks

And delightful dump trucks

And the fanciest doghouses you ever saw!

Dd

Did Doodle Draw That?

Initial sound /d/

Color and cut out a copy of the picture cards on page 22. Spread the cards facedown on the floor near your easel. Have your Doodle D. Dog puppet tell youngsters that he loves to draw pictures that begin with the letter *D!* Then have Doodle invite a volunteer to pick a card and name the picture. Next, have him lead youngsters in chanting the word to determine if it begins with /d/. If it does, have the child attach the card to the easel as Doodle says, "Yes, it does begin with *D!* That picture was drawn by me!" If it does not, have the child set the card aside as Doodle says, "No, it doesn't start with *D!* That picture wasn't drawn by me!" Continue in this manner with the remaining pictures.

Doodle D. Dog

Dog Treats for Doodle

Forming letter D

Encourage little learners to help prepare this delicious doggy snack! In advance, draw a large outline of the letter *D*. Obtain a dog bowl and a box of small dog treats (or dog bone cutouts). Have Doodle invite each youngster to place a few treats inside the outline of the letter. During each child's turn, have Doodle lead the group in chanting "/d/, /d/, /d/, /d/, dog bones!" When each student has had a turn, have youngsters place the dog treats in the bowl. Then invite Doodle to eat his favorite snack!

Doodle

Doodle D. Dog

TEC61113

Puppet Patterns
Use with "Doodle D. Dog" on page 18.

Picture Cards
Use with "Did Doodle Draw That?" on page 20.

Eggbert E. Egg

Materials for one puppet:

copy of the puppet pattern on page 26
business-size envelope
crayons
scissors
glue

Eggbert E. Egg

Directions

1. Color the cheeks on the puppet pattern.
2. Cut out the pattern.
3. Seal the envelope. Then cut the envelope in half.
4. Glue the egg cutout to an envelope half.

Eggbert E. Egg

Eggbert E. Egg
Can often be found
Riding in elevators,
Up and down.
In offices, hotels,
Or out at the mall,
Eggbert will be sure
To ride them all!

Eggbert's Egg Basket

Initial sound /ĕ/

To prepare for this activity, put a copy of each picture card from page 26 inside a different plastic egg and then place the eggs in a basket. Cut a sanitized egg carton in half so it will hold six eggs. Have your Eggbert E. Egg puppet invite a youngster to pick an egg from the basket. Have the child open the egg, remove the card, and name the picture. Use the puppet to engage students in evaluating the beginning sound of the word and deciding whether the word begins with /ĕ/. If it does, have the child put the card back inside the egg and then place the egg in the egg carton. If it does not, have him put the egg aside. Continue in the same manner until Eggbert's egg basket is empty and the egg carton is full!

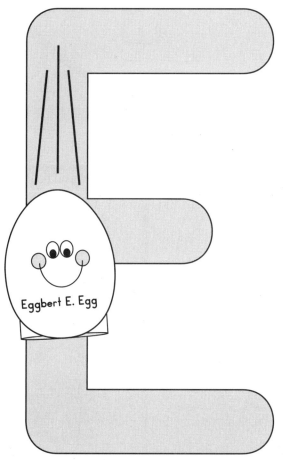

Eggbert E. Egg

An Elevator Ride!

Forming letter E

Eggbert E. Egg loves elevators, and he's ready for a supersize ride! Place an extra large *E* cutout on a wall. To begin, have your Eggbert E. Egg puppet ask a volunteer to take him for a ride on the *E* elevator. Have the child place the puppet at the top of the vertical line of the *E* and slide him to the bottom. Then have her place the puppet on the left side of the top floor (horizontal line) and slide him to the right. Have her repeat the process on the middle and bottom floors to finish Eggbert E. Egg's supersize elevator ride!

Puppet Pattern
Use with "Eggbert E. Egg" on page 23.

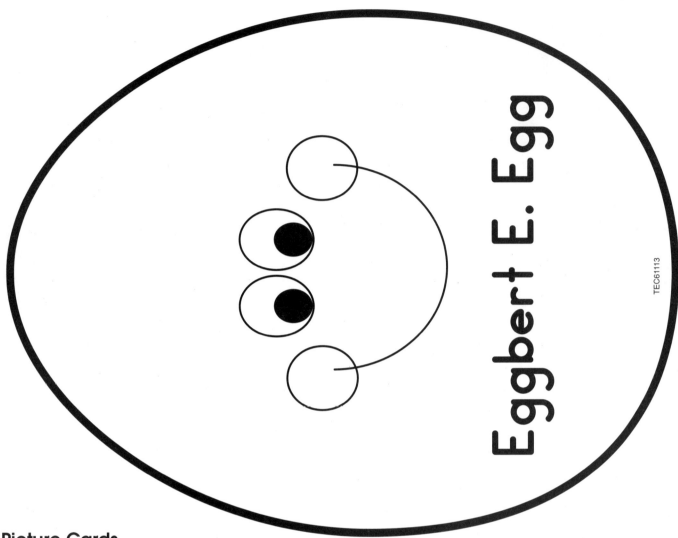

Eggbert E. Egg

TEC61113

Picture Cards
Use with "Eggbert's Egg Basket" on page 25.

F Fancy F. Fish

F F F F F F F F F F F F F F F F F F F F F F F F F F F F F F F F F F F F F F F F F F F F F

Materials for one puppet:

white construction paper copy
   of the pattern on page 30
jumbo craft stick
crayons
scissors
tape

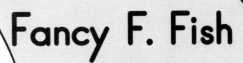

Directions

1. Color and cut out the pattern.
2. Tape the cutout to the craft stick to make the puppet shown.

F F F F F F F   F F F F F F F F F F F F F F F

Fancy F. Fish

Fancy F. Fish
Just couldn't be finer,
With her fluttering fins
And her tail behind her.
She swims with a swirl
Through the wide open sea,
Looking as pretty
As pretty can be!

Ff

Will Fancy Swim?

Initial sound /f/

Have each child make a Fancy F. Fish puppet as described on page 27. Give each child his puppet and then say a word. If the word begins with /f/, have youngsters move their puppets as if they are swimming through the sea. If the word does not begin with /f/, have students hold their puppets still. Continue in the same way with other words.

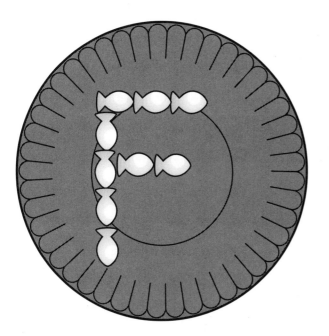

A Fishy F

Forming letter F

Have Fancy F. Fish encourage little learners to turn a yummy snack into the letter *F!* Give each child a blue paper plate on which you've written the letter *F* with permanent marker. Also give each child a handful of fish-shaped crackers. Instruct each child to place her crackers on the lines to form the letter *F.* Then have your Fancy F. Fish puppet encourage each child to say a word that begins with /f/ and "swim" a fish cracker into her mouth!

Fancy F. Fish

TEC61113

Alphabet Puppets From A to Z • ©The Mailbox® Books • TEC61113

Giggles G. Goat

Materials for one puppet:

copy of page 34
gray construction paper horns
lunch bag
crayons
scissors
glue

Giggles G. Goat

Directions

1. Color the puppet patterns.
2. Cut out the patterns and name card.
3. Glue the cutouts to the bag to make the puppet shown.
4. Glue the horns to the goat.

Giggles G. Goat

Giggles G. Goat thinks everything's funny.

He laughs when it's gloomy; he laughs when it's sunny.

He laughs in the morning; he laughs at night.

He laughs when he's eating, between every bite.

So the next time you hear "ha-ha" or "hee-hee,"

It just might be Giggles G. Goat that you see!

Gg

Giggles and Guffaws

Initial sound /g/

Gather youngsters and their Giggle G. Goat puppets for a giant round of laughter! Prepare several cards with words that begin with /g/ and a few other cards with words that begin with other sounds. Place the cards in a container. Have each child don his Giggles G. Goat puppet. Lead youngsters in reciting the rhyme shown. Then prompt a child to choose a card and hand it to you without showing the card to her classmates. Read the word aloud. If the word begins with /g/, instruct little ones to make their puppets giggle. If it doesn't, have youngsters keep their puppets silent. Continue choosing new volunteers until all the cards have been chosen.

Giggles is grumpy!
Oh no! It can't be!
Can we make him laugh?
We'll just have to see!

Giggles G. Goat

goat

fun

got

get

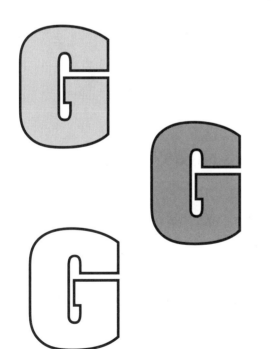

I See a G

Recognizing letter G

Have Giggles cheer little ones on as they hunt for the letter *G!* In advance, make a class supply of die-cut letter *G*s plus a few extras and hide them around your classroom. Begin the activity by walking around the room with Giggles, searching for a letter *G.* When Giggles finds a *G,* have him recite the chant shown. Then use Giggles to invite a few students at a time to walk around the classroom to each look for one letter *G.* When a student finds a *G,* she recites the chant and then takes her letter back to her seat. Continue in this manner until each child has found a letter.

Ha-ha! Hee-hee!
I see a letter *G!*

Puppet Patterns
Use with "Giggles G. Goat" on page 31.

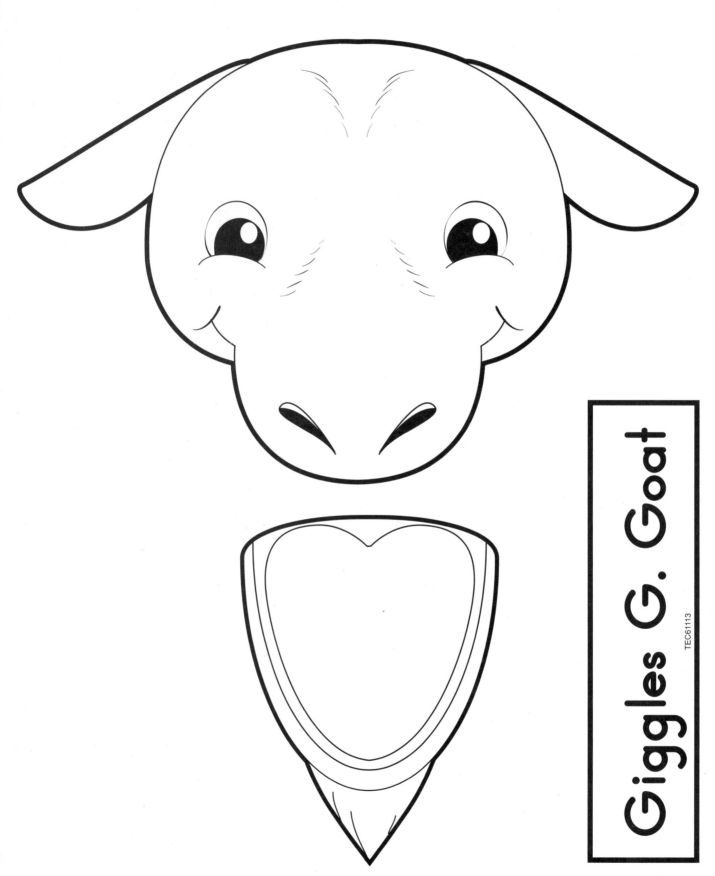

Giggles G. Goat

TEC61113

 **appy H. Hippo**

Materials for one puppet:

copy of page 38
lunch bag
crayons
scissors
glue

Happy H. Hippo

Directions

1. Color the puppet patterns.
2. Cut out the patterns and the name card.
3. Glue the cutouts to the bag to make the puppet shown.

Happy H. Hippo

Happy H. Hippo is special.

Happy H. Hippo is neat.

Happy H. Hippo can hop like a frog

On her big hippopotamus feet!

Hh

Hop Like Happy
Initial sound /h/

Get little ones hopping with Happy H. Hippo! Don your Happy H. Hippo puppet and have her introduce the activity by explaining how she immediately begins hopping whenever she hears a word that begins with the /h/ sound, just as her name does! Then direct students to stand and listen as you say a word. If the word begins with /h/, have youngsters hop with Happy. If it does not, have them stand very still. Continue in the same manner for several rounds.

Hat!

Happy H. Hippo

A Supersize *H*
Forming letter H

Help students hop their way to letter reinforcement with this gross-motor activity! Use masking tape to make an oversize letter *H* on the floor in an open area of the classroom. Then invite each child, in turn, to hold the Happy H. Hippo puppet as she hops along the lines of the letter.

Puppet Patterns and Name Card
Use with "Happy H. Hippo" on page 35.

Happy H. Hippo

TEC61113

I tsy I. Inchworm

Materials for one puppet:

construction paper copy of the
    puppet pattern and name
    card on page 42
jumbo craft stick
crayons
scissors
tape

Itsy I. Inchworm

Directions

1. Color the puppet pattern.
2. Cut out the puppet pattern and
    name card.
3. Tape the cutouts to the craft stick.

Itsy I. Inchworm

Itsy I. Inchworm is crawling along.

Itsy I. Inchworm is playing a song.

He plays tiny instruments;

He plays them quite well:

A trumpet, a drum set,

A small jingle bell.

He plays the flute and the tambourine.

He's the most musical inchworm you've ever seen!

I i

II

Play Along With Itsy
Initial sound /ĭ/

To begin, gather a small group of students and give each child an instrument. Then have your Itsy I. Inchworm puppet explain that he would like them to play the instruments, but only when they hear a word that begins with /ĭ/, just as his name does. Then call out words that begin with /ĭ/, along with words that do not. (See below for suggested words that begin with /ĭ/.) If a word begins with /ĭ/, have youngsters play their instruments. If it does not, have them hold the instruments still.

Suggested words:		
in	icky	insect
is	inch	itty-bitty
it	inside	infant
if	itchy	indoors

Oodles of Inchworms
Forming letter I

Have Itsy I. Inchworm inspire little learners to make the letter *I* with a simple craft material that looks just like him! To prepare, cut a supply of green pipe cleaners into short lengths. Give each child a sheet of construction paper labeled with the letter *I*. Instruct each child to spread a small amount of glue on the letter. Then have her move a piece of pipe cleaner onto the letter as if it were a crawling inchworm and place it on the glue. Instruct her to repeat the process until the letter is covered with inchworms! After each child is finished, have your Itsy I. Inchworm puppet show his excitement for a job well done.

IIIIIIIIIIIIIIIIIIIIIIIIIIIIIIIIIIIIIIIIIIIIIIIIIIII

Puppet Pattern and Name Card
Use with "Itsy I. Inchworm" on page 39.

Itsy I. Inchworm

TEC61113

Puppet Pattern
Use with "Jasper J. Jelly Bean" on page 43.

Jasper J. Jelly Bean

TEC61113

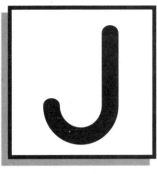

Jasper J. Jelly Bean

JJJJJJJJJJJJJJJJJJJJJJJJJJJJJJJJJJJJJ   JJJJJJJJJ

Materials for one puppet:

construction paper copy of the
    puppet pattern on page 42
jumbo craft stick
crayons
scissors
tape

Jasper J. Jelly Bean

Directions

1. Color the puppet pattern.
2. Cut out the pattern.
3. Tape the cutout to the craft stick,
   as shown, to make the puppet.

JJJJJJJJJJJJJ

Jasper J. Jelly Bean

Jasper J. Jelly Bean
Loves grape jelly!
He eats it and eats it
To fill his belly.
He's just as purple
As purple can be,
Because he's so full
Of grape jelly, you see!

44 *Alphabet Puppets From A to Z* • ©The Mailbox® Books • TEC61113

JJ

Top It With Jelly

Initial sound /j/

Only particular types of jellies top these bread cutouts! To prepare, cut out a construction paper copy of the jelly patterns on page 46. Cut out six construction paper bread shapes. Place the bread and jelly cutouts on the floor. Then gather youngsters around the cutouts. Have your Jasper J. Jelly Bean puppet prompt a child to look for a jelly cutout that shows a picture beginning with /j/. When he finds an appropriate cutout, have him place the jelly on a slice of bread. Continue in the same manner with each remaining jelly cutout, calling on a different youngster each time.

Jasper's Favorite Snack

Forming letter J

Youngsters are sure to enjoy this snack featuring Jasper J. Jelly Bean's favorite food. To begin, give each child a slice of bread. Provide grape jelly in squirt bottles and help each child squeeze a letter *J* on her bread. Use Jasper to lead youngsters in chanting, "/j/, /j/, /j/, /j/, Jasper loves jelly!" while forming the letter. Then have your Jasper J. Jelly Bean puppet encourage each child to name other words that begin with *J* as she enjoys her delicious snack.

JJJJJJJJJJJJJJJJJJJJJJJJJJJJJJJJJJJJJJJJJJJJJJJJJJ

Jelly Patterns

Use with "Top It With Jelly"
on page 45.

TEC61113

TEC61113

TEC61113

TEC61113

TEC61113

TEC61113

TEC61113

TEC61113

Kiki K. Kite

Materials for one puppet:

contrasting construction paper copies of the kite
    and bow patterns (page 50)
curling ribbon
jumbo craft stick
scissors
stapler
glue
tape

Kiki K. Kite

Directions

1. Cut out the kite
   and bow patterns.
2. Join several lengths of curling
   ribbon together by knotting them
   at one end. Then staple the
   knotted end of the curling ribbon to the bottom of the kite.
3. Glue the bow to the kite so it covers the staple.
4. Tape the kite to a jumbo craft stick.

Kiki K. Kite

Look, way up high!
What is that in the sky?
Why, it must be
Kiki K . Kite flying by!
She bobs and she twirls
And she dances around.
And she blows lots of kisses
To kids on the ground.

K k

Kisses for Kiki

Initial sound /k/

Kiki K. Kite blows lots of kisses; now it's her turn to get some back! To begin, hold your Kiki K. Kite puppet and gather students in your large-group area. Explain to students that they will each blow a kiss to Kiki when they hear a word that begins with /k/. If they hear a word that does not begin with /k/, they will not blow kisses. Say the word *key* and prompt students to blow kisses to Kiki. Then continue in a similar way, alternating the words shown with words that do not begin with /k/.

Suggested words:

kiss	kin	kitten	kangaroo	keep	kind
kettle	kick	king	karate	key	kayak

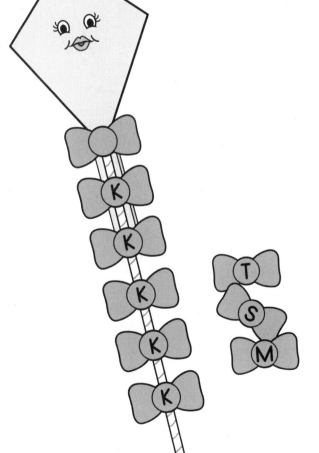

Kiki's Fancy Tail

Letter knowledge

Cut out several copies of the bow pattern on page 50. Label the majority of the bows with the letter *K* and the remaining bows with different letters. Remove the curling ribbon from the Kiki K. Kite puppet and attach a length of yarn to make a long tail. Place the puppet at the table along with the supply of bows. A youngster visits the center and chooses a bow. If the bow shows the letter *K*, she places the bow on the tail. If it does not, she puts the bow in a separate pile. She continues in this fashion with each remaining bow.

Kite Pattern
Use with "Kiki K. Kite" on page 47.

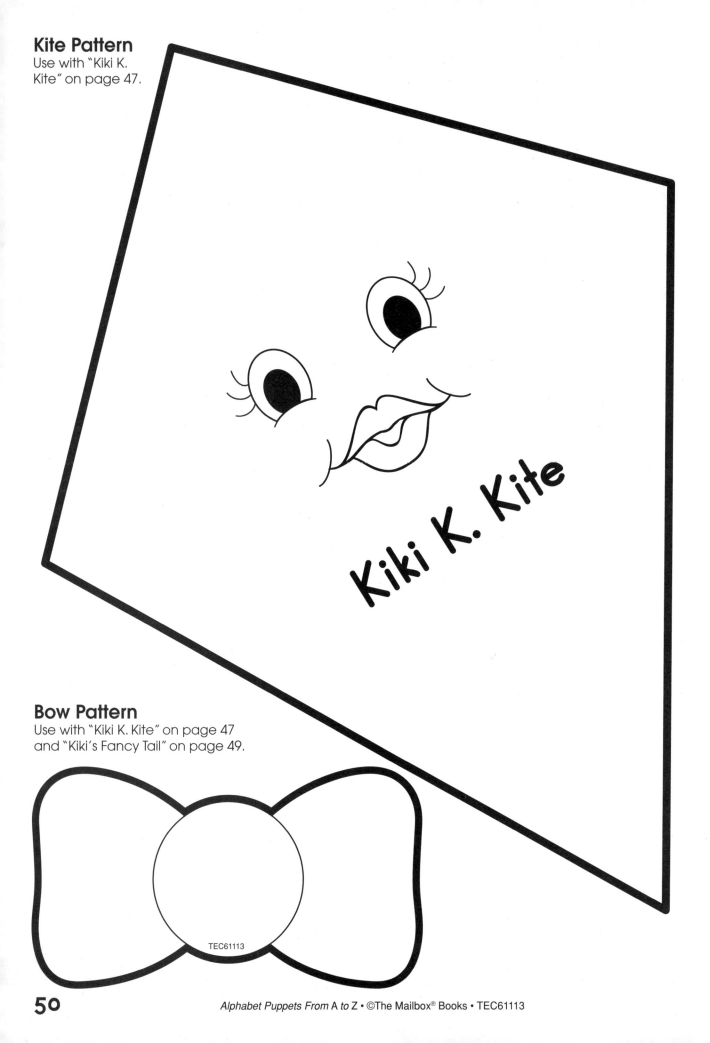

Kiki K. Kite

Bow Pattern
Use with "Kiki K. Kite" on page 47
and "Kiki's Fancy Tail" on page 49.

TEC61113

L

Lulu L. Ladybug

LLLLLLLLLLLLLLLLLLLLLLLLLLLLLLLLLLLLLLLLLLLLLL

Materials for one puppet:

copy of the name card on page 54
2 large paper plates
black sock
construction paper eye cutouts
crayons
stapler
hot glue gun (for teacher use)

Lulu L. Ladybug

Directions

1. Draw pupils on the eye cutouts and then hot-glue the cutouts to the toe of the sock.
2. Color the back of one paper plate so it resembles a ladybug's body.
3. Glue the name card to the colored paper plate.
4. Staple the edges of the two paper plates together, leaving openings on opposite sides of the plates as shown.
5. Glue the strips to the plates to make legs.
6. Slip the black sock onto your hand and then slide your hand through the openings.

LLLLLLL LLLLLLL

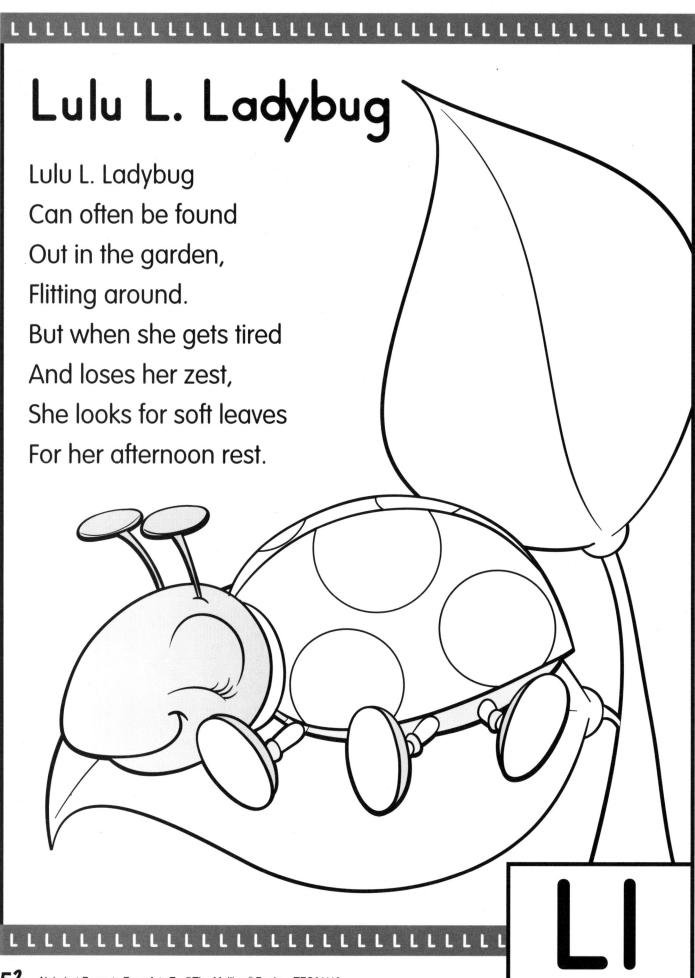

Lulu L. Ladybug

Lulu L. Ladybug
Can often be found
Out in the garden,
Flitting around.
But when she gets tired
And loses her zest,
She looks for soft leaves
For her afternoon rest.

Ll

Lulu's Snooze

Initial sound /l/

Cut out a copy of the leaves on page 54. Obtain a shallow container or box. To begin, have your Lulu L. Ladybug puppet explain that she loves to nap on nice soft leaves and that her favorite leaves show pictures that begin with /l/, just as her name does! Then invite a child to choose a leaf. If the leaf shows a picture whose name begins with /l/, have him put it in Lulu's leaf container. If it does not, have him set it aside. Continue in the same way with all the remaining leaves. Then have Lulu "crawl" into the container for her afternoon nap.

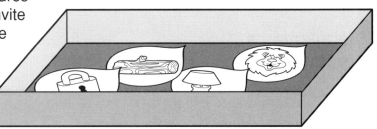

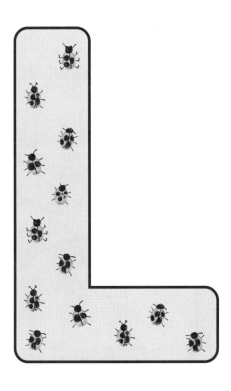

Ladybugs Aplenty

Forming letter L

Have your Lulu L. Ladybug puppet show great enthusiasm as youngsters create these fingerprint ladybugs! Prepare a class supply of construction paper *L* cutouts. Have Lulu invite each child to trace his *L* with his hand and say its name. Then prompt the child to press a fingertip onto a red ink pad and make prints on his cutout. Next, have the youngster transform each fingerprint into a ladybug by using a fine-tip black marker to add a head, legs, and spots.

Name Card
Use with "Lulu L. Ladybug" on page 51.

Lulu L. Ladybug

TEC61113

Leaf Patterns
Use with "Lulu's Snooze" on page 53.

Alphabet Puppets From A to Z • ©The Mailbox® Books • TEC61113

Monty M. Moose

Materials for one puppet:

construction paper copy of
    pages 58 and 59
paper lunch bag
crayons
scissors
glue

Monty M. Moose

Directions

1. Color the puppet patterns.
2. Cut out the patterns and the name card.
3. Glue the antlers to the back of the head.
4. Glue the cutouts to the bag, as shown, to make the puppet.

Monty M. Moose

Monty M. Moose
Is a marvelous fellow.
His favorite food
Is the mini marshmallow.
He likes them in cocoa
And on pie and ice cream.
And when Monty sleeps,
He has marshmallow dreams!

Mm

Fill the Mug
Initial sound /m/

Invite little ones to help make Monty M. Moose's favorite beverage—a moose-size cup of cocoa with marshmallows! In advance, cut an oversize mug shape from poster board. Also make a supply of marshmallow cutouts. Have your Monty M. Moose puppet explain to children that he is going to say some words, and each time they hear a word that begins with /m/, he wants them to add a marshmallow to the cup. Have Monty say a word. (See below for suggested /m/ words.) If the word begins with /m/, have a volunteer attach a marshmallow to the cup. If it does not, have the class chant, "No marshmallows for Monty!" as Monty gives a very disappointed sigh. Continue until Monty's cup is brimming with marshmallows.

Suggested words:

mat	mail	mouse	mop
mitten	mud	moon	map
man	monkey	mask	middle

Marvelous Marshmallows
Forming letter M

Give each child a sheet of construction paper programmed with an outline of the letter *M*. Provide a shallow container of white paint, along with a supply of large marshmallows. Have each child dip a marshmallow in the paint and then make marshmallow prints on the letter *M*. After a desired effect is achieved, have your Monty M. Moose puppet show his delight for the youngster's masterpiece. After all, marshmallows are Monty's favorite food!

Monty M. Moose

TEC61113

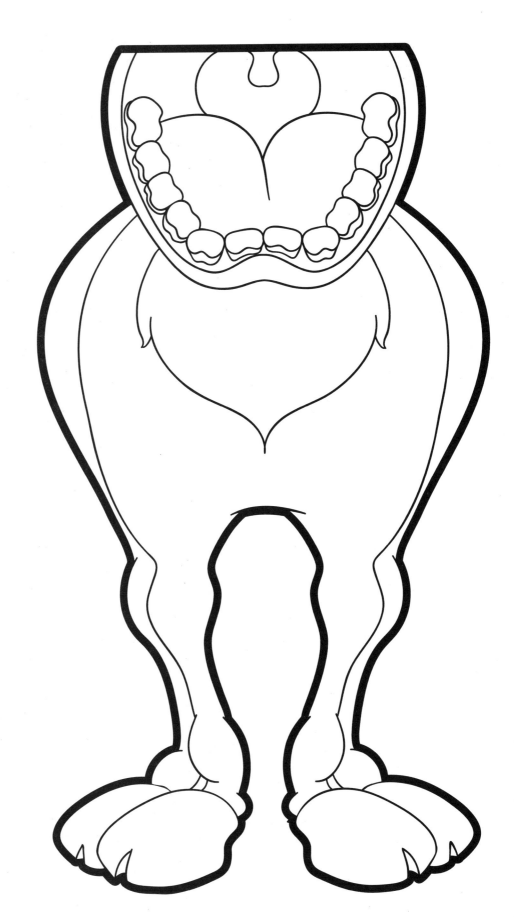

 **utty N. Nutcracker**

Materials for one puppet:

copy of the puppet pattern on page 63
business-size envelope
crayons
scissors
glue

Directions

1. Color and cut out the puppet pattern.
2. Seal the envelope. Then cut off one end of the envelope to make an opening for your hand.
3. Glue the cutout to the envelope, as shown, to make the puppet.

Nutty N. Nutcracker

Nutty N. Nutcracker doesn't like nuts.

He just will not crack them, no ifs, ands, or buts.

Instead Nutty really enjoys eating noodles.

He eats them all day—he eats oodles and oodles!

Noodles in the morning, at noon, and at night,

Nutty thinks noodles are just out-of-sight!

Nn

Nutty's Noodles

Initial sound /n/

To prepare for this activity, put dry egg noodles in a cooking pot. Gather a medium bowl and a large spoon. Cut out a copy of the picture cards on page 63 and then put the cards in the empty noodle bag or box. To begin, have your Nutty N. Nutcracker puppet explain to students how he wants to have a bowl of noodles for lunch, but he needs help removing the noodles from the pot and placing them in the dish. Next, invite a volunteer to pick a card and name the picture. Have Nutty N. Nutcracker lead the class in deciding if the word begins with /n/. If it does, have a child add a spoonful of noodles to the bowl. If it does not, have youngsters chant, "No noodles!" After all the cards have been chosen, invite Nutty N. Nutcracker to eat his noodles!

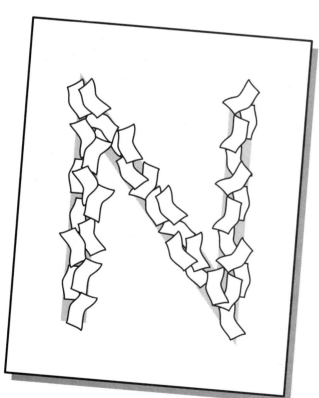

Oodles of Noodles

Forming letter N

Give each child a sheet of construction paper labeled with a large letter *N.* Have your Nutty N. Nutcracker puppet invite each student to glue dry noodles along the letter lines, prompting her to say the /n/ sound as she works. After each child completes her work, post the project so Nutty N. Nutcracker can admire this nifty noodle art!

Puppet Pattern
Use with "Nutty N. Nutcracker" on page 60.

Nutty N. Nutcracker

TEC61113

Picture Cards
Use with "Nutty's Noodles" on page 62.

TEC61113

TEC61113

TEC61113

TEC61113

TEC61113

TEC61113

Octavia O. Octopus

Materials for one puppet:

copy of the puppet patterns
    on pages 67 and 68
large paper plate, cut in half
crayons

scissors
glue
stapler

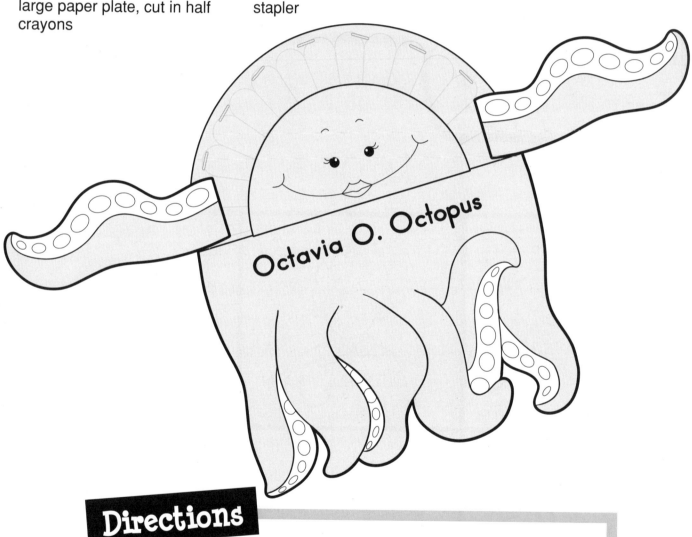

Directions

1. Color and cut out the puppet patterns.
2. Color the outside of the plate halves.
3. Glue the face and tentacles to a plate half as shown.
4. Staple the plate halves together, leaving the straight sides open to put your hand in.

Octavia O. Octopus

Octavia O. Octopus is as strong as an ox!

She can easily lift a one-hundred-pound box.

Why is it so heavy?

Oh what could be in it?

Open it up; it'll just take a minute.

It's filled with olives—her favorite meal.

Octavia can lift them; it's no big deal!

THIS
↑ SIDE ↑
UP

O o

Octavia's Lunch
Initial sound /o/

Bring to your circle-time area a supply of green pom-poms (olives) and a lunchbox (or other container). Don your Octavia O. Octopus puppet and have her tell students that she is very hungry, but she has run out of olives and her lunchbox is empty! Then read aloud a list of words that begin with the /o/ sound, along with some that do not. (See below for suggested /o/ words.) If a word begins with /o/, as in Octavia's name, invite a volunteer to put an olive in Octavia's lunchbox. If it does not, lead the class in chanting, "No olive for Octavia!" At the close of the activity, have Octavia O. Octopus thank youngsters for helping her as she lifts her lunchbox with great dramatic flair!

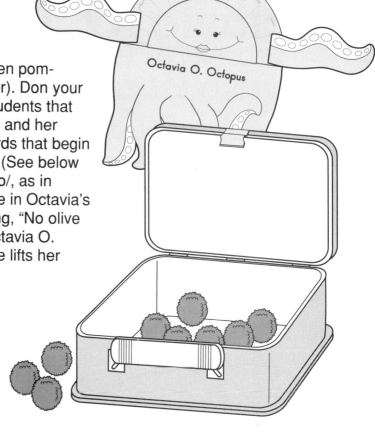

Octavia O. Octopus

Suggested words:		
odd	olive	on
oblong	octopus	object
obvious	October	opera

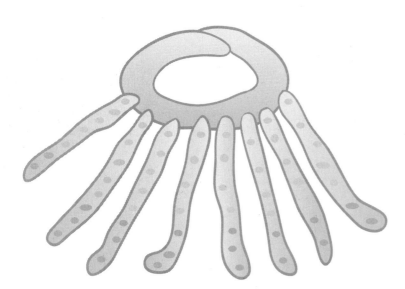

An *O* of Dough
Forming letter O

Help each child turn a portion of play dough into an Octavia O. Octopus of a different kind! Use your Octavia O. Octopus puppet to encourage each child to roll her dough into a snakelike shape. Have her bend the shape into a letter *O* and then fasten the ends together to make Octavia's body. Prompt each child to run her fingers over the dough and say the letter's name. Next, have her use the remaining dough to fashion eight tentacles and attach them to Octavia's body. Then have your Octavia puppet show enthusiastic approval for a likeness of her that is so well done!

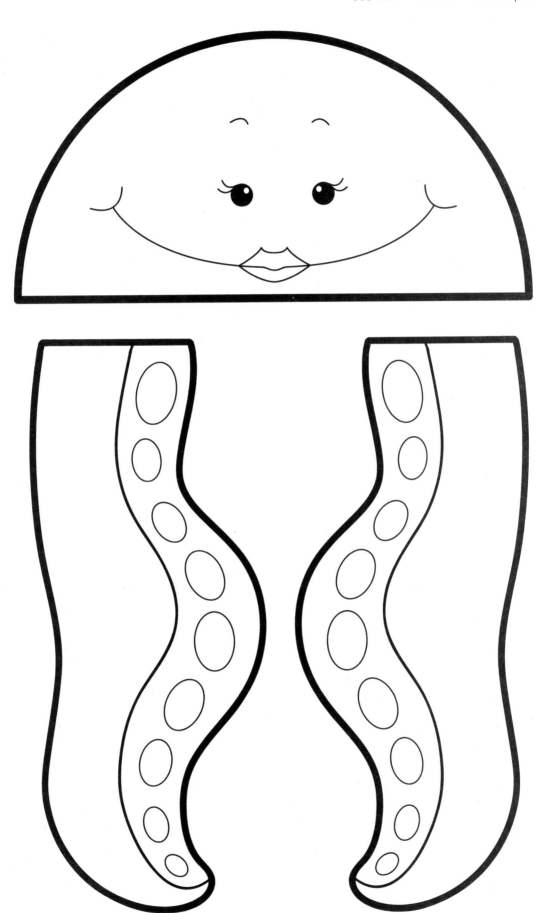

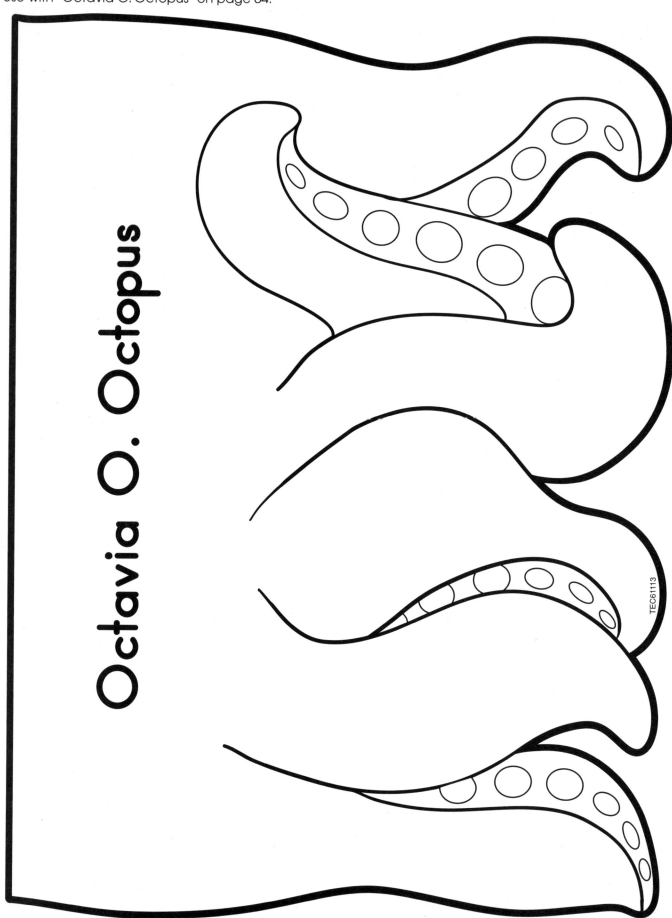

Octavia O. Octopus

TEC61113

Pippy P. Penguin

Materials for one puppet:

white construction paper copy of page 72
jumbo craft stick
crayons
scissors
tape

Pippy P. Penguin

Directions

1. Color the puppet pattern, making the hat purple and the scarf pink.
2. Cut out the pattern and the name card.
3. Tape the cutouts to the craft stick.

Pippy P. Penguin

Pippy P. Penguin
Loves purple and pink.
She looks so stunning
At the skating rink!
Purple hat, pink scarf,
And oh! Polka dots!
Pippy loves purple and pink
Quite a lot!

P p

Pippy's Polka Dots

Initial sound /p/

Color and cut out a copy of the cards on page 73; then place the cards in a bag. Cut out seven large pink and purple circles and scatter them on the floor so they resemble polka dots. Have your Pippy P. Penguin puppet explain to children that she wants to go ice-skating but can't until each polka dot is decorated with a picture whose name begins with /p/, just as her name does. Then have Pippy choose a volunteer to pick a card from the bag. Have youngsters name the picture and decide whether the name begins with /p/. If it does, have the child place the card on a polka dot. If it does not, have him set the card aside. Continue in the same fashion until each polka dot has a picture. Then encourage each child, in turn, to skate with Pippy around the polka dots!

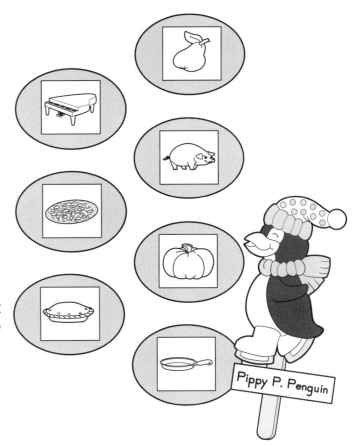

Pippy P. Penguin

/p/, /p/, pink!
/p/, /p/, purple!
/p/, /p/, Pippy
Loves polka dots!

A Pink and Purple *P*

Forming letter P

Pippy P. Penguin just loves polka dots made with pink and purple ink! Give each youngster a sheet of white construction paper labeled with the outline of a large letter *P*. Provide bingo daubers with pink and purple ink and invite each child to decorate her letter with colorful polka dots. Have Pippy lead youngsters in the chant shown as they decorate.

Puppet Pattern and Name Card

Use with "Pippy P. Penguin" on page 69.

Pippy P. Penguin

TEC61113

TEC61113

TEC61113

TEC61113

TEC61113

TEC61113

TEC61113

TEC61113

TEC61113

TEC61113

Quinella Q. Queen

Q Q Q Q Q Q Q Q Q Q Q Q Q Q Q Q Q Q Q Q Q Q

Materials for one puppet:

copy of the puppet patterns on page 77
construction paper strips
construction paper hand cutouts
lunch bag
crayons
scissors
glue

Directions

1. Color and cut out the puppet patterns.
2. Glue the strips to the head to make hair.
3. Glue the hand cutouts to the quilt.
4. Glue the cutouts to the bag as shown, making sure the upper and lower lips line up correctly.

Quinella Q. Queen

Quinella Q. Queen
Has a needle and thread.
She's making a blanket
To go on her bed.
Quickly she sews up
A quilt oh so warm
To keep herself cozy
In any snowstorm.

Qq

Alphabet Puppets From A to Z • ©The Mailbox® Books • TEC61113

A Quilt of Qs

Initial sound of the letter Q

Have Her Majesty, Quinella Q. Queen, guide youngsters as they make this mini quilt. Give each student a nine-inch construction paper square folded into four sections, as shown, along with a copy of the picture cards on page 85. Use your Quinella Q. Queen puppet to help each child determine which pictures begin like *quilt.* Then instruct him to color the appropriate cards. Next, have him cut out the colored cards and glue each one to the prepared paper as shown. To finish this royal masterpiece, have Quinella encourage each child to put a decorative border around each picture card.

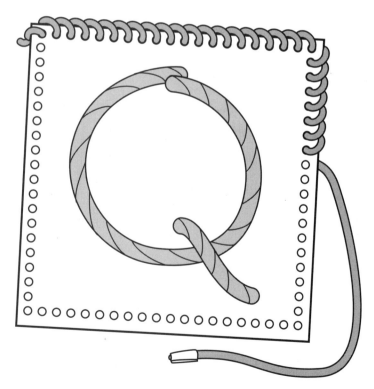

Lovely Stitching

Forming letter Q

Cut a square from poster board and label it with the letter *Q.* Then laminate the poster board for durability. Glue a length of yarn to the outline of the letter. After the glue dries, punch holes around the edges of the square and then tie a length of yarn to one of the holes. Wrap a small piece of tape around the remaining end of the yarn to keep it from fraying. Use your Quinella Q. Queen puppet to invite each youngster, in turn, to trace the *Q* with her finger and then use the attached yarn to sew around the edges of the square. After each child is finished, have Quinella Q. Queen compliment her on a job well done.

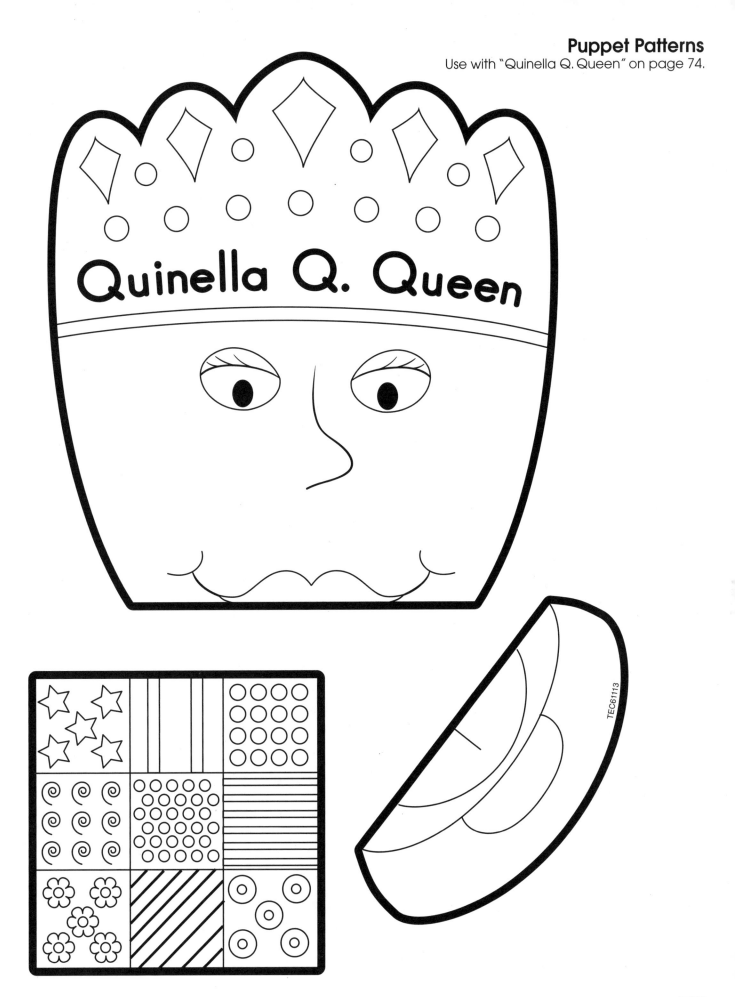

Quinella Q. Queen

ocky R. Robot

RRRRRRRRRRRRRRRRRRR   RRRRRRR

Materials for one puppet:

copy of the puppet patterns on page 81
2 construction paper strips
envelope
crayons
scissors
glue
tape

All About
Rainbows

Rocky R. Robot

Directions

1. Color and cut out the patterns.
2. Seal the envelope; then cut off one end of the envelope to make an opening for your hand.
3. Accordion-fold the strips and then tape them to the robot to make arms.
4. Glue the robot to the envelope.
5. Tape the hand and book cutouts to separate arms.

RRRRRRRRR   RRRRRRR

Rocky R. Robot

Roses
Rocks
Reindeer

Rocky R. Robot loves to read

About roses and rocks and reindeer, indeed.

But his favorite thing to read about

Has to be rainbows, without a doubt!

He loves their colors—yes, this is true.

He would love to read about rainbows to you!

All About
Rainb

R r

Alphabet Puppets From A to Z • ©The Mailbox® Books • TEC61113

Rocky Reads

Initial sound /r/

With this small-group activity, little ones make a book that Rocky would love! To prepare, color and cut out a copy of the picture cards on page 81. Also prepare a small blank six-page booklet with a cover, titled as shown. Introduce the Rocky R. Robot puppet and remind students that Rocky likes to read about things with names that begin with /r/. Hold up a picture card and invite students to name the item. Lead youngsters to determine whether the word begins with /r/. If it does, ask a child to glue it to a page in Rocky's book. If the item's name begins with a different sound, set it aside. Continue in the same manner with each remaining card.

Rocky's R Words

All About Rainbows

Rocky R. Robot

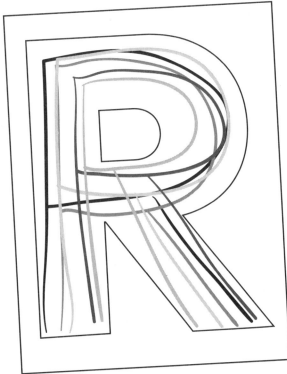

A Rainbow R

Forming letter R

Reinforce the formation of the letter _R_ by having youngsters color it so it resembles Rocky's favorite thing—a rainbow! Outline the letter _R_ on a sheet of paper. Then make a copy of the paper for each child. Have each youngster trace the inside of the _R_ several times, each time with a different crayon color. While students are working, use the puppet to praise them for their hard work!

Rocky R. Robot

TEC61113

All About Rainbows

Picture Cards
Use with "Rocky Reads" on page 80.

TEC61113

TEC61113

TEC61113

TEC61113

TEC61113

TEC61113

TEC61113

TEC61113

Sally S. Sunshine

Materials for one puppet:

copy of the puppet pattern
    and name card on page 85
paper plate
jumbo craft stick
crayons
scissors
glue
tape

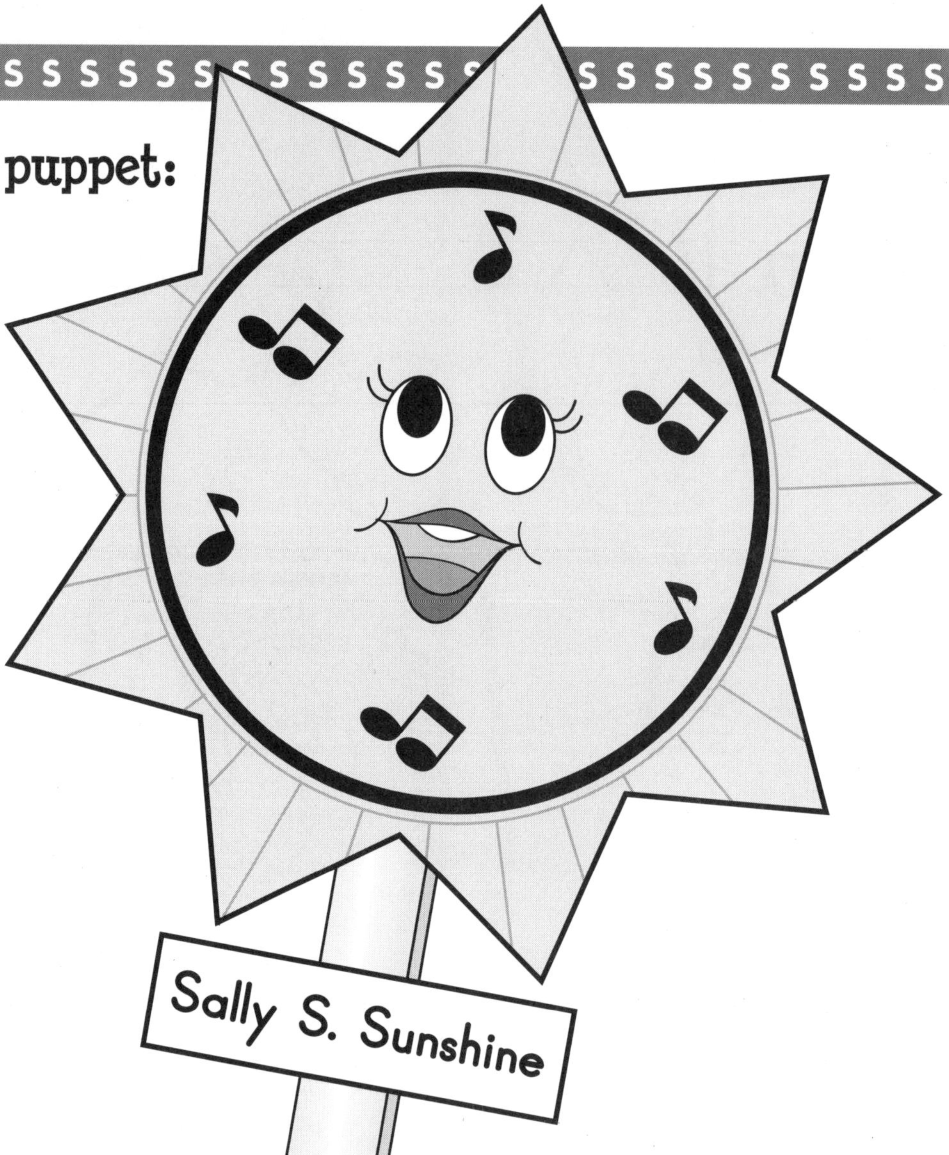

Sally S. Sunshine

Directions

1. Color the puppet pattern.
2. Cut out the pattern and name card.
3. Cut points around the edges of the plate so it resembles a sun.
4. Glue the cutouts to the plate as shown.
5. Tape the craft stick to the back of the plate to complete the puppet.

Sally S. Sunshine

Sally S. Sunshine likes to sing

Silly old songs about anything!

She sings about seeds and summer and socks.

She sings to the trees; she sings to the rocks.

So next time you see her way up in the sky,

She just might be singing a soft lullaby.

S s

Sing for Sally

Initial sound /s/

Gather youngsters for circle time and bring along your Sally S. Sunshine puppet. Explain that not only does Sally like to sing, but she likes to listen to children sing as well! Read aloud a list of words, including many that begin with /s/ (see words that begin with /s/ below). Pause after each word. If a word begins with /s/, youngsters sing, "So, so, so." If the word begins with a different sound, they remain quiet. Have Sally sway to the music as little ones sing at the appropriate times.

So, so, so!

Suggested words:

sun	sink	sound
safe	sip	so
send	sit	see
size	sort	sand

S Is for Sun

Recognizing letter S

To prepare for this group activity, label a large yellow paper circle and a supply of yellow triangles with the letter S. Also label a few yellow triangles with other letters. Post the circle on a wall or bulletin board and place the triangles facedown nearby. Invite a child to choose a triangle and determine whether the letter is S. If it is S, she uses Sticky-Tac to attach the triangle to the sun so it resembles a ray from the sun. If it is not S, she sets it aside. Have Sally sing a note or two to reward each child's correct choice.

Sally S. Sunshine

TEC61113

Picture Cards
Use with "A Quilt of Qs" on page 76.

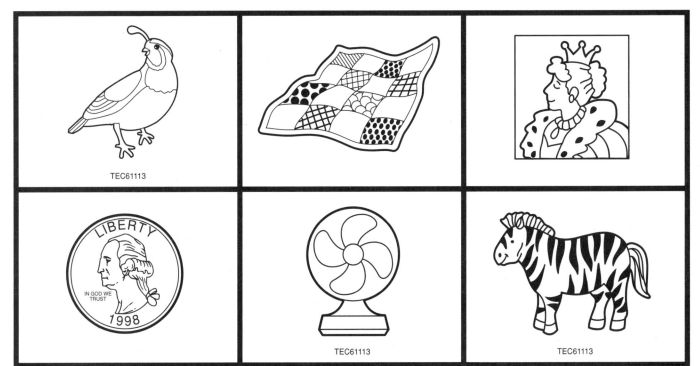

TEC61113

TEC61113

TEC61113

Tickle T. Turtle

Materials for one puppet

copy of the puppet patterns and
  name card on page 89
large paper plate half
construction paper feet and tail
jumbo craft stick
crayons
scissors
glue
tape

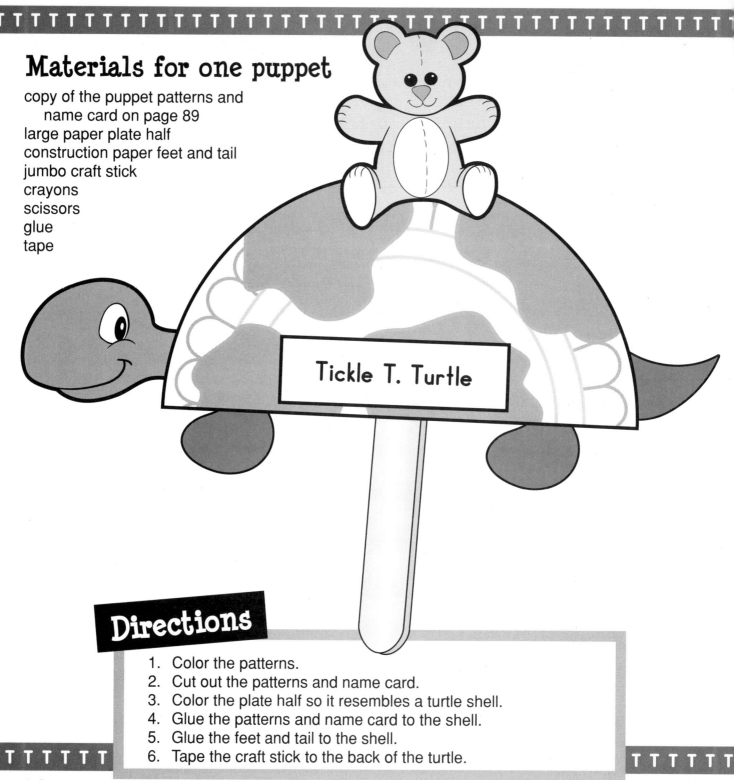

Tickle T. Turtle

Directions

1. Color the patterns.
2. Cut out the patterns and name card.
3. Color the plate half so it resembles a turtle shell.
4. Glue the patterns and name card to the shell.
5. Glue the feet and tail to the shell.
6. Tape the craft stick to the back of the turtle.

Tickle T. Turtle

Tickle T. Turtle
Has a tan teddy bear.
He carries it on
His shell everywhere.
Teddy's with Tickle
All day and all night.
Tickle loves Teddy
With all his might!

T t

Tickle's Shell

Initial sound /t/

Students add pictures whose names begin with /t/ to Tickle T. Turtle's shell. To prepare, draw a simple turtle outline on a sheet of paper to represent Tickle T. Turtle; then copy the paper to make a class supply. Give each child a prepared paper and a copy of the picture cards on page 89. Invite her to color the turtle. Then have her say the names of the picture cards, leading her to understand that all the names begin with /t/. Instruct her to color and cut out the cards and then glue them to Tickle's shell. Don't forget to have each student draw Tickle's friend Teddy on top of the shell!

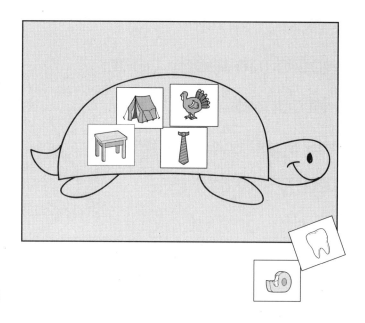

Turtle Crawl

Forming letter T

Not only is this gross-motor activity fun, but it reinforces the letter *T*. Use masking tape to create an extra large *T* on the floor. Have youngsters identify the letter. Then invite each child, in turn, to crawl along the letter while balancing a teddy bear on his back, just as Tickle T. Turtle does! When he completes the letter, have your Tickle T. Turtle puppet congratulate him on a job well done!

Tickle T. Turtle

TEC61113

Picture Cards
Use with "Tickle's Shell" on page 88.

TEC61113

ncle U. Umbrella

Materials for one puppet:

copy of the puppet patterns and name card
    on page 93
large paper plate half
jumbo craft stick
crayons
scissors
glue
tape

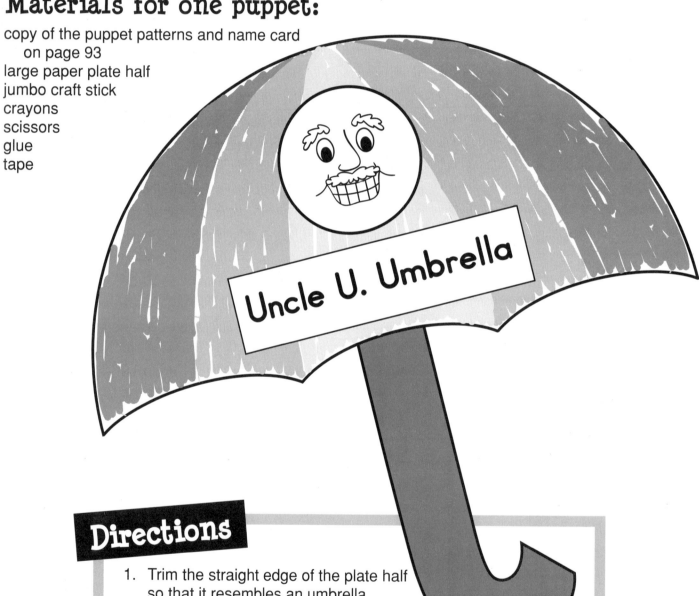

Uncle U. Umbrella

Directions

1. Trim the straight edge of the plate half so that it resembles an umbrella.
2. Color the umbrella.
3. Cut out the patterns and name card.
4. Glue the face and name card to the umbrella.
5. Glue the umbrella handle to the craft stick.
6. Tape the handle to the back of the umbrella.

Uncle U. Umbrella

What should you do when it's raining,

When you don't want to get wet?

Call Uncle U. Umbrella

Because he's your very best bet!

With Uncle U. Umbrella,

You're bound to stay nice and dry.

And when the rain has ended,

Just say, "Thank you!" and "Goodbye!"

U u

Under the Umbrella

Initial sound /ŭ/

Only words that begin with /ŭ/ can stay dry under Uncle U. Umbrella! Color and cut out a copy of the picture cards on page 93. Post your Uncle U. Umbrella puppet on a wall within students' reach. Gather a small group of students around the puppet. Then show a picture card and have youngsters name the picture. Encourage students to determine whether the name begins with /ŭ/, like the word *umbrella*. If it does, invite a child to tape the card below the umbrella. If it begins with a different sound, have the child set the card aside. Continue in the same manner for each remaining card.

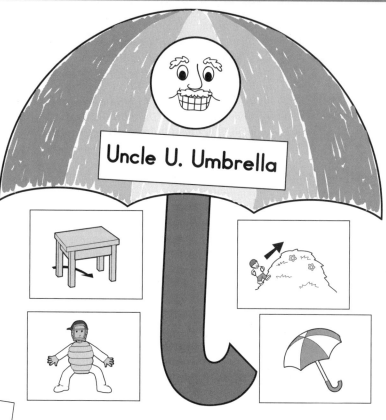

Umbrella Spin

Recognizing letter U

Put a spin on learning the letter *U* with this circle-time game! Prepare a set of letter cards, many of which are labeled with letter *U*. Seat students in a circle and place a closed umbrella in the center. Invite a child to carefully spin the umbrella. When the umbrella stops, hold up a letter card. The child sitting opposite the umbrella handle stands up if the letter is a *U*. If it is a different letter, the child remains still. Then invite that child to spin the umbrella to play again.

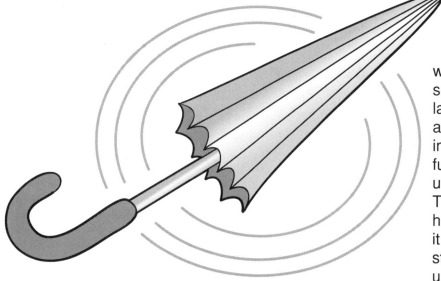

Uncle U. Umbrella

TEC61113

Victor V. Vine

TEC61113

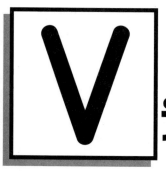

Victor V. Vine

Materials for one puppet:

copy of the name card on page 93
green sock
2 eye cutouts
3 green pipe cleaners
green craft foam leaves
hot glue gun (for teacher use only)

Victor V. Vine

Directions

1. Hot-glue the eye cutouts to the toe end of the sock.
2. Twist the pipe cleaners together end to end to make one length.
3. Wrap the long pipe cleaner around the sock, hot-gluing it to the sock as you go so the pipe cleaner resembles a vine. (Make sure it's wrapped loose enough to allow your hand to slide into the sock.)
4. Hot-glue the leaves to the vine.
5. Hot-glue the name card to the sock.

Victor V. Vine

Victor V. Vine
Is a plant that can climb.
It climbs to the top
Of a wall in no time!
The top of the wall
Has the very best view
Of violets in purple—
The loveliest hue!

V v

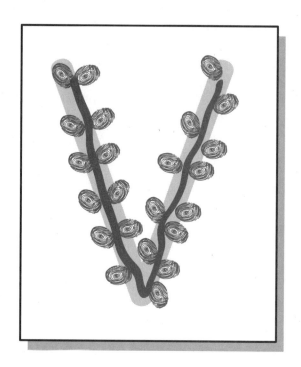

A V-Shaped Vine
Forming letter V

Have your Victor V. Vine puppet watch little ones make a *V* look like a vine! Draw a large *V* on a sheet of paper; then copy the paper to make a class supply. Have each child use a thick green marker to trace the letter while he says the letter's name. Then invite him to add green fingerprint leaves to the letter so that it resembles a vine.

A Very Tall Wall
Initial sound /v/

Little ones help Victor climb a wall while listening for the /v/ sound! On a sheet of bulletin board paper, draw a wall with six rows of bricks. Don your Victor V. Vine puppet and say a word. (See the list for several /v/ words.) Ask students to determine whether the word begins with /v/, as Victor's name does. If it does, hold Victor up to the first row of bricks. If it begins with a different sound, do not move Victor. Continue announcing words, moving Victor up a row each time a /v/ word is heard. When Victor reaches the top of the wall, invite students to celebrate the victory!

Suggested words:

vase	violin
very	vacuum
van	vote

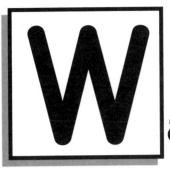

Walter W. Walrus

Materials for one puppet:

copy of page 100
paper lunch bag
crayons
scissors
glue

Walter W. Walrus

Directions

1. Color the puppet pattern.
2. Cut out the pattern and name card.
3. Glue the pattern to the flap of the lunch bag.
4. Glue the name card on the puppet.

Walter W. Walrus

I looked in the water
And what did I see?
Walter W. Walrus was
Waving at me!
He wiggled his tusks
And he winked his eye.
Then he raised a flipper
And waved goodbye!

W w

Wink, Walter!

Initial sound /w/

To prepare for this small-group activity, shape blue yarn into a circle that is large enough for a small group of youngsters to stand in. Invite a group of students to stand in the circle (water) and explain that Walter W. Walrus likes to be winked at when he hears words that begin with the same sound as his name. Hold up your Walter puppet and announce a word. (See the suggestions below for /w/ words.) If the word begins with /w/, prompt students to wink at Walter. If it begins with a different sound, have youngsters remain still. Continue play in the same manner for several rounds; then invite students to wave goodbye to Walter!

will

Suggested words:

win	will	want
with	we	wish
well	wall	watch
worm	walk	wig

W-w-w-waves

Letter/sound association

Encourage each child to draw a picture on a sheet of white paper of Walter W. Walrus. Then provide a *W* stamp and a blue ink pad. Have each child stamp *W*s on his paper repeatedly to create waves. Prompt him to say the /w/ sound each time he makes a stamp. What wonderful waves!

Puppet Pattern and Name Card
Use with "Walter W. Walrus" on page 97.

Walter W. Walrus

ton X. X-ray

x x x x x x x x x x x x x x x x x x x x x x

Materials for one puppet:

copy of the puppet pattern and name card
    on page 104
jumbo craft stick
scissors
glue
tape

Xton X. X-ray

Directions

1. Cut out the puppet pattern and the name card.
2. Glue the name card to the puppet as shown.
3. Tape the craft stick to the back of the puppet.

x x x x x x x x x

Xton X. X-ray

Xton X. X-ray
Is an excellent guy.
He's extra friendly
And always waves hi!
He loves to help
Whenever he can.
Then everyone shouts,
"Xton's our man!"

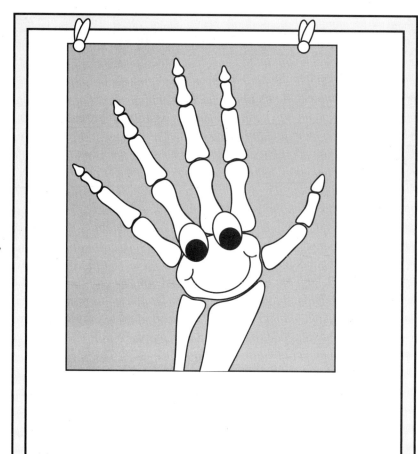

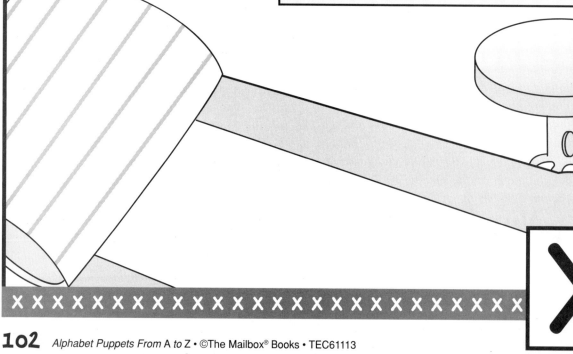

Xx

Wave Like Xton

Sound of the letter X

Invite youngsters to bring their Xton X. X-ray puppets to circle time. Instruct each child to lay his puppet on the floor in front of him and pretend it is sleeping. Explain to students that Xton X. X-ray likes to take naps, but whenever he hears a word with the sound /ks/ of the letter *X*, he wakes up and waves hello! Then read aloud a list of words that contain the sound of *X,* along with words that do not. For each word that contains the sound, a student picks up his puppet and moves it as if it's waving. For words that do not, he leaves Xton X. X-ray asleep on the floor, and the group quietly says, "Shhhh." To conclude the activity, encourage each child to turn to a classmate and use the Xton X. X-ray puppet to give a high five for a job well done!

Xton X. X-ray

Suggested words:			
box	fix	tax	six
wax	ax	relax	nix
fox	fax	mix	ox

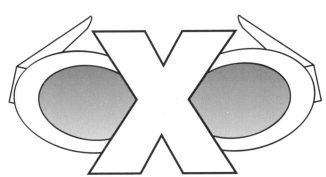

"X-tra" Special Glasses

Recognizing letter X

To prepare for this group activity, obtain a few pairs of children's sunglasses. Copy and cut out a class supply of the letter *X* on page 104 plus enough extras to attach one *X* to each pair of sunglasses. Place the remaining *X*s throughout the classroom. Have your Xton X. X-ray puppet invite volunteers to each put on a pair of glasses and walk around the room in search of a letter *X.* After each child locates an *X,* use your puppet to instruct her to return to her seat with her letter *X* in hand. Continue in the same fashion until each child has used a pair of the special glasses to help her find an *X.*

Puppet Pattern and Name Card
Use with "Xton X. X-ray" on page 101.

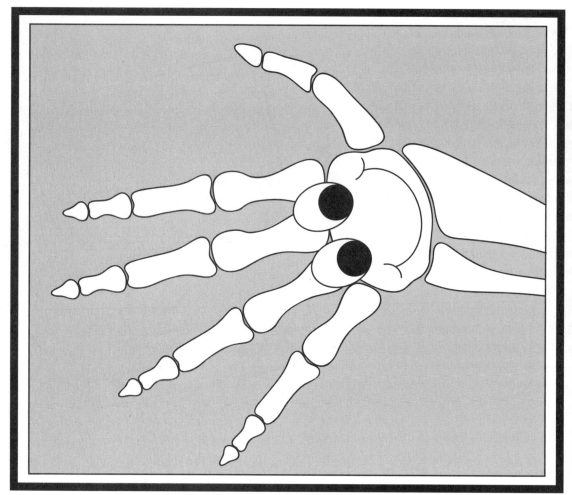

Xton X. X-ray

TEC61113

Letter *X* Pattern
Use with "'X-tra' Special Glasses" on page 103.

TEC61113

Yakety Y. Yak

Materials for one puppet:

construction paper copy of page 108
construction paper horns
lunch bag
brown yarn pieces
crayons
scissors
glue

Yakety Y. Yak

Directions

1. Cut out the puppet patterns and the name card.
2. Glue the horns to the back of the head.
3. Glue the cutouts to the bag to make the puppet shown.
4. Glue yarn to the puppet so that it resembles hair.

Yakety Y. Yak

Yakety Y. Yak just loves to talk
When he stands on the mountain
Or goes for a walk!
He talks all day long,
And he talks in his sleep.
But when he is eating,
You won't hear a peep!

Yy

Yeah or Yawn?
Initial sound /y/

In advance, obtain a telephone to use as a prop. Don your Yakety Y. Yak puppet and explain to students that Yakety is awaiting a phone call. When he gets the call, he will hear words that will help the class learn about the sound of the letter *Y.* Have Yakety Y. Yak answer the phone when it rings, listen for a moment, and then call out a word. Use the puppet to engage the class in evaluating the word's beginning sound. If the word begins with /y/, lead students in saying "Yeah!" accompanied by a round of applause. If it does not, lead youngsters in giving a big yawn and then have the puppet fall asleep! Encourage little ones to call for Yakety Y. Yak to wake up; then continue the activity in the same manner as before.

Yes!

Yakety Y. Yak

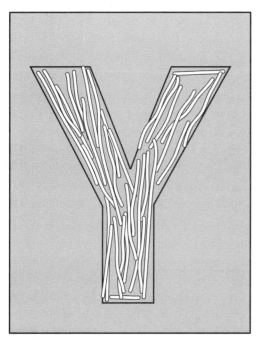

A *Y* of Yellow Yarn
Letter-sound association

To prepare, cut a supply of yellow yarn into different lengths. Give each child a sheet of construction paper programmed with an outline of the letter *Y.* Then have your Yakety Y. Yak puppet instruct each student to glue lengths of the yarn inside the outline. As they work, use the puppet to lead youngsters in chanting, "/y/, /y/, yellow yarn!" Once the completed artwork is dry, have Yakety Y. Yak encourage each little learner to trace the tactile *Y* with her fingers.

Puppet Patterns and Name Card
Use with "Yakety Y. Yak" on page 105.

Yakety Y. Yak

Zowie Z. Zebra

ZZZZZZZZZZZZZZZZZZZZZ   ZZZ

Materials for one puppet:

copy of page 112
lunch bag
crayons
scissors
glue

Zowie Z. Zebra

Directions

1. Color the puppet patterns.
2. Cut out the patterns and the name card.
3. Glue the cutouts to the bag to make the puppet shown.

ZZZZZZZZ   ZZZZZZZ

z z z z z z z z z z z z z z z z z z z z z z z z z z z z z z z z z z z z

Zowie Z. Zebra

Zowie Z. Zebra lives at the zoo.

In his zebra zone there's plenty to do!

He can zoom 'cross the grass,

Zigzag through the trees,

Or zip into the shade

to catch a few Zzzz's!

Zowie

z z z z z z z z z z z z z z z z z z z z z z z z z z z z z z z z z z z z

Zz

Zooming for Zs
Initial sound /z/

Gather students in a large open space for this fun and engaging activity. To begin, have your Zowie Z. Zebra puppet tell little ones how he loves to zoom around the zoo. Explain to youngsters that *zooming* means "going really fast." Use the puppet to instruct students to zoom from one location to another if they hear a word that begins with /z/. If they hear a word that does not begin with /z/, they should stand still. (See the list below for words that begin with /z/.) Then call out a word and watch the zooming begin!

Suggested words:			
zipper	zoo	zucchini	zone
zero	zip	zebra	zap

zipper

A Zigzag Z
Forming letter Z

Have Zowie Z. Zebra on hand to help guide youngsters as they make this striped *Z!* To prepare, cut a supply of black rickrack ribbon into different lengths. Give each child a sheet of construction paper labeled with a large outline of the letter *Z*. Have your Zowie Z. Zebra puppet invite little learners to glue pieces of rickrack within the outline of the *Z*. As each child completes her project, have Zowie Z. Zebra zigzag around the table to show his excitement for a job well done!

Puppet Patterns and Name Card

Use with "Zowie Z. Zebra" on page 109.

Zowie Z. Zebra

TEC61113